Contents

Welcome to Japan!

Hello! My name is Benjamin Blog and this is Barko Polo, my **inquisitive** dog. (He is named after ancient ace explorer, **Marco Polo**.) We have just got back from our latest adventure – exploring Japan. We put this book together from some of the blog posts we wrote on the way.

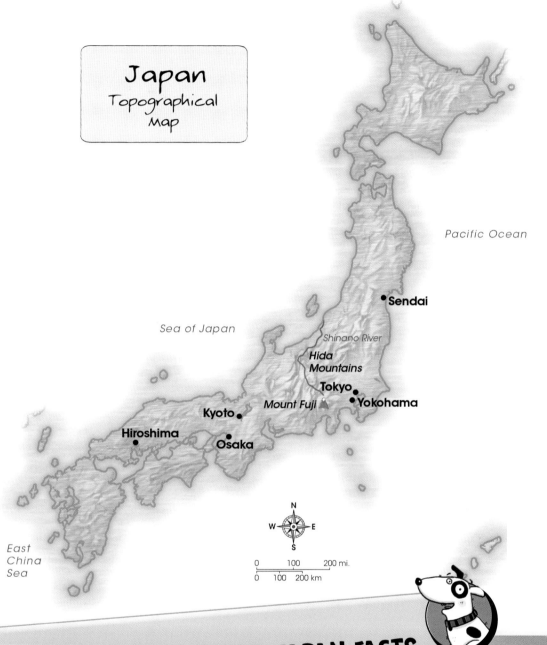

Japan
Topographical
Map

Pacific Ocean

• Sendai

Sea of Japan

Shinano River

Hida Mountains

Tokyo
Mount Fuji • **Yokohama**

Kyoto •

Hiroshima

Osaka

N
W   E
S

0   100   200 mi.
0   100   200 km

East China Sea

BARKO'S BLOG-TASTIC JAPAN FACTS

Japan is a long, thin country in eastern Asia. It is made up of more than 6,000 islands in the Pacific Ocean – four large ones and lots of smaller ones.

Samurai and emperors

Our first stop was the museum in Tokyo where we saw this amazing suit of **armour**. It belonged to a Japanese warrior, called a **samurai**. The samurai were skilled in **martial arts**, **archery**, and sword fighting. For hundreds of years, they were very powerful fighters in Japan.

BARKO'S BLOG-TASTIC JAPAN FACTS

The Imperial Palace in Tokyo is the home of the **emperor** of Japan. The emperor's birthday is 23 December, so there are many people here, waving Japanese flags.

Islands, earthquakes, and mountains

Posted by: Ben Blog | 3 January at 2.30 p.m.

The four largest islands in Japan are Honshu, Hokkaido, Shikoku, and Kyushu. From Tokyo (on the island of Honshu), we headed south to Shikoku. You can hop from island to island by ferry or tunnel, but we decided to take the motorway across this enormous bridge.

BARKO'S BLOG-TASTIC JAPAN FACTS

Hundreds of earthquakes strike Japan every year. In 2011, the worst quake in Japanese history hit Honshu. It set off a terrible **tsunami**, and thousands of people died.

Back in Honshu, we stopped to see the amazing Mount Fuji. At 3,776 metres (12,388 feet), it is the highest mountain in Japan. It is also a volcano, although it has not erupted for years. In summer, many people climb it at night to be at the top when the sun rises.

BARKO'S BLOG-TASTIC JAPAN FACTS

These snow macaques keep extra warm in winter by taking a dip in a hot spring. The warm water and steam are heated up by hot rocks under the ground.

Busy cities

Posted by: Ben Blog | 2 February at 11.25 p.m.

Today, we arrived back in Tokyo, the capital of Japan. Around 13 million people live here, so it is pretty crowded. On the subway, there are special "people pushers" to squeeze people on to trains so that the doors can close. Yikes! I think I will do my exploring on foot.

BARKO'S BLOG-TASTIC JAPAN FACTS

High-speed bullet trains carry passengers between Japan's big cities. They can race along at speeds of 310 kilometres (192 miles) per hour and travel from Tokyo to Osaka in around two hours.

Konnichiwa!

Posted by: Ben Blog | 6 March at 4.11 p.m.

Konnichiwa means "hello" in Japanese, which is the language spoken in Japan. When people meet, they also bow to each other to show **respect**. In Japan, it is very important to be polite and show respect to others, especially if they are older than you are.

BARKO'S BLOG-TASTIC JAPAN FACTS

Most Japanese people wear western-style clothes, such as jeans and T-shirts. Some people wear **kimonos**, like this one, on festivals and other special occasions.

In Japan, going to school is very important, and children work hard from a young age. School days are long, and pupils often stay behind to help clean their classrooms after school. At primary school, children study maths, science, and Japanese.

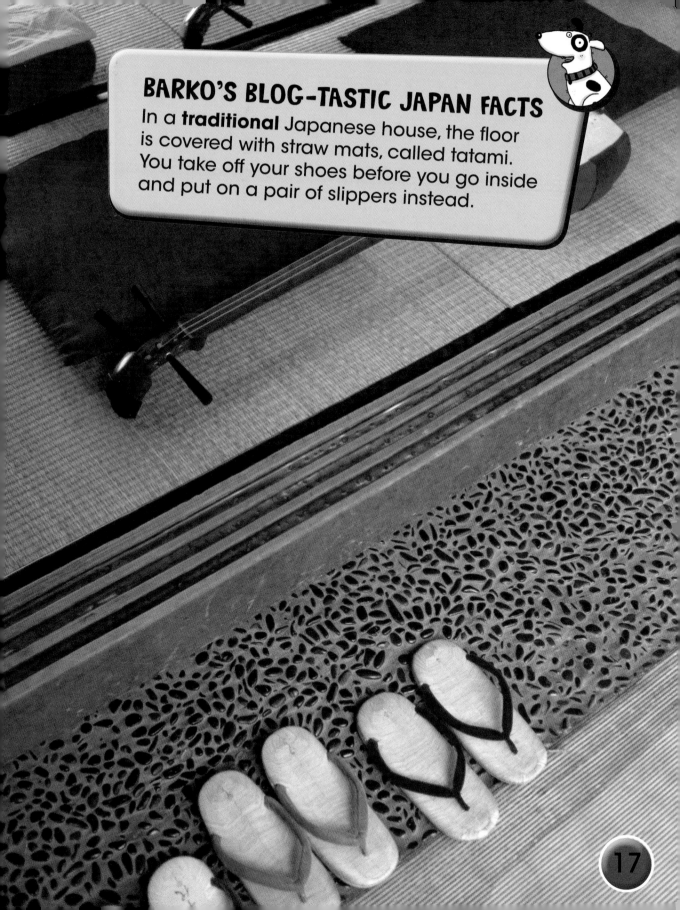

BARKO'S BLOG-TASTIC JAPAN FACTS

In a **traditional** Japanese house, the floor is covered with straw mats, called tatami. You take off your shoes before you go inside and put on a pair of slippers instead.

Our next stop was the city of Kyoto, which is famous for its Shinto **shrines**. Shinto is a religion followed by many people in Japan. They believe in spirits that exist in nature, animals, and people. They worship the spirits in beautiful shrines, like this one.

BARKO'S BLOG-TASTIC JAPAN FACTS

In spring, a special celebration takes place in Japan. All over the country, people go to see the cherry trees as they start to blossom. They hang lanterns from the branches and have picnics and parties under the trees.

Anyone for sushi?

Posted by: Ben Blog | 25 May at 6.37 p.m.

After all that sightseeing, we were hungry. We stopped at a restaurant to try some sushi. Sushi is raw fish mixed with rice and sometimes rolled up in seaweed. It is very popular in Japan. People also eat noodles, soup, and deep-fried vegetables in batter, called tempura.

BARKO'S BLOG-TASTIC JAPAN FACTS

In Japan, making tea is an ancient **tradition**. A special ceremony is held to make, serve, and drink the tea. It takes several years to learn how to do everything in the right order.

Sport and leisure

Posted by: Ben Blog | 19 June at 1.17 p.m.

In their spare time, Japanese children like to read comic books, called manga. Some of these comics are turned into films. People also enjoy karaoke – singing their favourite songs to music. Barko wanted to try it, but I have the latest manga to read.

BARKO'S BLOG-TASTIC JAPAN FACTS

The most popular sport in Japan is sumo. Two wrestlers try to throw each other on to the ground or force each other out of the ring. It sounds much too tiring for me!

From car factories to fish markets

Posted by: Ben Blog | 30 July at 10.37 a.m.

While we were in Sendai, I stopped to visit this car factory. Japanese cars are sold all over the world. The cars are built by human workers and by robots. Japan is also famous for making **electronic goods**, such as MP3 players, cameras, and TVs.

BARKO'S BLOG-TASTIC JAPAN FACTS
The Tsukiji Fish Market in Tokyo is the biggest fish market in the world. Japanese boats catch around 7 million tonnes of fish every year.

And finally ...

It is the last day of our trip, and I am here in Hiroshima visiting the Peace Memorial. In 1945, during World War II, an atomic bomb was dropped on the city. More than 70,000 people were killed instantly. This was one of the few buildings to survive the deadly blast.

27

Japan fact file

Area: 377,915 square kilometres
(145,914 square miles)

Population: 127,253,075 (2013)

Capital city: Tokyo

Other main cities: Yokohama; Osaka

Language: Japanese

Main religions: Shinto; Buddhism

Highest mountain: Mount Fuji
(3,776 metres/12,388 feet)

Longest river: Shinano
(367 kilometres/228 miles)

Currency: Yen

Japan quiz

Find out how much you know about Japan with our quick quiz.

1. How many islands make up Japan?
a) more than 100
b) more than 6,000
c) four

2. What is a **kimono**?
a) a Japanese dress
b) a Japanese drink
c) a Japanese train

3. What is sushi made from?
a) raw fish
b) raw meat
c) cooked rice

4. What are Japanese comics called?
a) karaoke
b) manga
c) sumo

5. What is this?

Answers
1. b
2. a
3. a and c
4. b
5. Himeji Castle

29

Glossary

archery shooting with a bow and arrow

armour a suit made of metal worn to protect a person when fighting

electronic goods machines that use electricity, such as televisions and computers

emperor a ruler

inquisitive being interested in learning about the world

kimono a long, loose robe with wide sleeves

Marco Polo an explorer who lived from about 1254 to 1324; he travelled from Italy to China

martial art a kind of sport, such as judo or karate

respect being polite and helpful to someone else

samurai a type of Japanese warrior

shrine a holy place where people worship or place holy objects or images

tradition something that has been done the same way for many years

tsunami a huge wave that causes terrible flooding if it hits the land

30

Find out more

Books

Japan (Countries in Our World), Jim Pipe
(Franklin Watts, 2012)

Japanese (Languages of the World),
Harriet Milles (Raintree, 2013)

We Visit Japan (Your Land and My Land),
Tammy Gagne (Mitchell Lane Publishers, 2013)

Websites

kids.nationalgeographic.com/kids/places
The National Geographic website has lots of
information, photos, and maps of countries around
the world.

www.worldatlas.com
Packed with information about various countries,
this website includes flags, time zones, facts, maps,
and timelines.

Index